The King's ⌐
is Missing!

Written by
Cath Jones

Illustrated by
Leo Trinidad

Ransⵙm

The king had his best crown on.

He **did** look important!

Then there was a big gust of wind, and it took his crown right off!

Up, up into the air it went.

It fell on to a black cat – and the cat ran off with the crown!

"Help! Help!" said the king.
He was so upset!

Now he did not look at all
important!

"Quick! I need my crown back!"
he said.

The queen said, "I will summon
that clever owl. He might get the
crown for us."

Tap! Tap! Tap! Owl sprang into the room!

The owl said, "I have come to help!"

"Wow! That was quick," said the king.

"I will hunt for the crown," said the owl.
"To start, I will track down that cat."

But the cat did not have the crown!

"I did not keep that crown. It was
much too bright," said the cat.
"A little rabbit has the crown now."

Owl set off to track down
the little rabbit.

But the little rabbit did not
have the crown!

"That crown got stuck on my ears!
I did not keep it!" the little rabbit
said. "So my mum got rid of it in
the river!"

Just then, some fish swam near them.
One of the fish had the crown on!

"Get that fish!" said Owl.

Then a big shark swam up the river.

"Stop! No!" said the owl to the shark.
"Do not gulp that fish!"

Munch, slurp, gulp!

Plop! Ping!

The shark spat the crown
on to the river bank.

"Yuck!" said the shark.
"That is horrid!"

The crown was all right. It just had a little dent – and some shark spit on it.

"You are so clever, Owl," said the king. "Thanks for getting back my crown."

"No problem," said the clever owl. "But I think it might need a bit of a scrub!"